CLAW

WAY BACK...

Surviving bereavement

By Joyce Lesley Keating

A lot of this has personal relevance as I lost my husband,Jim, three years ago. There was input from Revd Mark Cantrill of the Clays group of Anglican churches, and close friend Rosemary Hall, a worship leader in the Methodist church.

Pictures used are all from the Creative Commons website and are copyright free. Many thanks.

NOW WHAT?

Spent in bouts of weeping interspersed with numbness, legalities and paperwork, the time between the death and the funeral is over. The visitors who came with you to the church or crematorium have eaten the last few pieces of cake and gone home.

This is when the well-meaning advice of family and friends begins to roll in. (Either that or they can't talk to you at all because this is a new and alien experience for them, and they can't imagine what to say.) Unfortunately, some of the advice is like the directions to the traveler, you know, the famous ones:

"Well, if I were you, I wouldn't start from here…"

But, like all journeys, you are stuck with the starting point of this one. It is how you *feel* here and now, and how you claw your way back to something you can live with.

That is my hope, that in sharing a little of the help I was given, I can ease your journey.

SEA OF EMOTION

A turbulent personality might possibly be used to being overwhelmed by emotion. But suppose you are usually more buttoned up? Is there a way to make some kind of sense of it all? If you have lost a partner, a family member or close friend, as well as thinking you have been abandoned, there are other swirling emotions threatening to drown you.

In my case, my husband, Jim, went through several years of the slow decay of Parkinson's Disease. Latterly there was the anguish of watching someone I loved deteriorate into a shell I barely recognized. By the time I held his hand for his last breath, my first reaction was relief that the agony was over, both for him and for me.

Then came the guilt. How wrong and unnatural was it to welcome death that way? It wasn't. It could only be good that the suffering was not prolonged.

I have talked with others whose loss was sudden, from a stroke, an accident, or a heart attack, and discovered another strange feeling accompanies that kind of loss. Anger. That might be directed at the person themselves for going, or a person of faith might direct the anger response towards God for taking them. Again, don't *suppress* it, *express* it. Shout, throw things, if it helps. (Stick to the rubbish china, not the priceless Ming vase!)

I cannot even begin to imagine the anger felt by families of those who were victims of murder. Try www.victimsupport.org.uk or phone 08081689111

Perhaps you missed the last few hours and felt you did not say a proper goodbye. Because writing is my obsession, my first thought is to write it down. Perhaps a letter, however scrappy, could capture what you would have wanted to say. Sometimes just pouring it all out eases the burden a little. It can be kept, burnt, buried, or turned into a boat and floated on the river or the sea. That way, those pent-up feelings would be expressed and released.

More difficult to deal with are the emotions of those who have lost a child, a baby, or gone through the trauma of a miscarriage. The loss of the hoped-for future is made more poignant because there is little or no past to cherish. Who knows what skills and talents are lost to the world? For these deaths, more than any other, counselling and professional help can make a difference. Your GP may be able to suggest the right person. Try CRUSE for bereavement counselling

www.cruse.org.uk or phone them on 0808 808 1677

Talking to Samaritans can help

www.samaritans.org or phone them on116123 anytime of the day or night. If you can express yourself better in an email get in touch with them on jo@samaritans.org for a reply within 24 hours.

Some people find that it helps to plant a rose, or a young sapling as a living, growing reminder of the young life lost. Others begin a blog of the journey out of despair. Another way is to support or work for charities which aim to find a cure for the illness which snatched away the little one. Perhaps a group could be started up in the child's name to raise funds in support of disease research or for a children's ward. These would all be a lasting legacy in your child's name.

If you have turned to faith to sustain you, why not contact a minister from one of your local faith groups? They are used to helping people in this kind of situation.

David Adams in "Tides and Seasons" gives a little Celtic poem which can act as a prayer for these bleak "Desert times"

"Desert Waters"

O spring in the desert

O shelter from the heat

O light in the darkness

O guide for the feet

O joy in our sadness

O support for the weak

O Lord with us always

Your presence we seek.

DEALING WITH THE SILENCE

You may be lucky enough to be living with a large family. If so, silence may not be your problem. If you find yourself longing for quiet and a chance to get your head together, try to designate a space where the rest of your family know they are not to follow and interrupt. A cook I knew who had a large family and no time to herself used to sit in a certain chair and throw her apron over her head and everyone knew it was better to tiptoe away and manage their crisis themselves…

During my husband's long illness, we spent all our time together. My only break was when a carer came for two hours each week to enable me to go out. So, when he was finally admitted to hospital and then a care home there was a lot of adjusting to be done. At first, the empty house and the silence felt awful.

I couldn't bear to listen to music as familiar tunes we had shared together made the loss worse. It is only now, three and a half years later that I have begun to enjoy listening to our favourite folk and classical pieces again. I began with pop music on radio two because he hated that and I knew there would be no reminders.

So, the TV went on in the morning at breakfast time and I switched it off as I went to bed. Again, it is only recently that I have begun to enjoy the peace of my home and the TV goes off unless there is something I really want to see.

I did wonder if having a pet again would help as we had kept cats in the past. Then I realized my mobility problems would make this difficult. But if you are fit enough it can be a great answer to loneliness and silence. Likewise, a friend (who had also been left alone) and I thought of teaming up and sharing a house. Luckily, we worked out in time how much we like our independence and how badly we would clash. In fact, I now love living alone and see my home as a refuge not a prison. (That has even been the case during the corona virus lockdown.)

It all depends on what kind of personality we are blessed with and the solution we find needs to allow for this. So, as with everything else after bereavement, take time to discover yourself and your own way forward. Are you the kind of person who only comes alive among a crowd? Or, do you feel at your best alone on a country path or beside a quiet lake?

Good friends help. I have a couple of people who ring me or I ring them every day. They also went shopping with me or out for a meal. If you don't drive, don't let that keep you in. Walk more or use public transport. It may be that if it is your partner who died you feel you would like, after a time, to meet someone new. Don't feel guilty. After all, if you had been the one to die you would not have wanted your partner to stay alone and miserable.

PRACTICAL PROBLEMS

Experiencing loss is exhausting. You may have been "running on empty" for a long time. Only now do you realize how exhausted you are.

SLEEP

As soon as you settle to sleep, everything starts racing round in your head. You toss about and feel more wide- awake than when you were watching the news. (You may have actually nodded off at that point.)

What's to be done? Firstly, DON'T rely on substances such as sleeping tablets, drugs, or alcohol. Sooner or later you have to stop their use (and that may be difficult as they are all addictive) but then you find the problem has not gone away, it may even be worse. Of course, your doctor may have prescribed something to help for a while but try not to prolong its use. There are a few things which helped me.so I pass them on:

- During the day get out in the sunshine if there is any. Indoors have as much bright light as possible until mid- evening then use dim lighting only. This lets your body know you are ready for sleep. Try to stick to the same times each day for going to bed and getting up. A pattern like this conditions the body.
- Try not to use a laptop, phone or tablet just before going to bed as the light prevents your brain from winding down.
- Some people find a hot milky drink at bedtime helps as milk contains L-

Tryptophan. This gets your body to produce melatonin and serotonin encouraging sleep.

- Then, when you lie down and the thoughts and feelings start up again, promise yourself that you can think about them all in the morning. Some people of faith turn them all over to God. Try to relax and breathe deeply and slowly (Let your chest come up on the in-breath and allow your chest to sink in on the out breath which should take a little longer). Keep your mind empty.

If you wake in the night, do it all again.

FOOD

When you are hurting so much inside it is hard to be bothered to make a meal. You do need fuel to keep you going but preferably not just biscuits and chocolate.

If you can't get out to get things or haven't the energy to cook there are ready made meals you can have delivered.

If you are elderly or disabled, ask your doctor about meals on wheels or try the meals at home service via the government website:

www.gov.uk/mealsathome

Younger people can access meals commercially by way of other providers, such as

Wiltshire farm foods if you have freezer space:

www.wiltshirefarmfoods.com or phone 0800 066 3502

or,

www.oakhousefoods.co.uk

Meals which are vacuum packed and store in an ordinary cupboard can be had from Parsley Box:

www.parsleybox.com or phone 0800 612 7225

Try to get as much fruit, vegetables and salad as you can. Vary what you get and find ones you can enjoy.

FINANCE

If you have always been the one to organize finance for the household, you may already be ahead of the game.

Even if this is the case, were you prepared for your income to halve itself overnight? Perhaps you never liked numbers so your partner did it all. Worse, if your partner was a control freak you may never have seen the paperwork at all.

Suddenly there is a deluge of information, possibly even debts that you had no idea about. There may be unpaid bills and final demands suddenly dropped on you. Housing or rent may be a problem.

DON'T PANIC...

This is the time to call in the experts who have seen it all before. This is more common than you think. A useful first stop is the Citizens' Advice Bureau

www.citizensadvice.org.uk or phone 03444 111 444

to find your local advice centre where they can help you sort out your next step.

You can also find some financial support on the following website

www.gov.uk/bereavement-support-payment

If you can't access the internet yourself ask a family member or friend to do it for you.

Your local bank branch can also offer sympathetic and confidential advice.

Pensions. They need to know your partner has died. Contact

www.gov.uk/contact-pension-service

or ring 0800 7310469 (Mon to Fri 9.30am to 3.30pm)

The website has a step-by-step guide.

Be aware that other "Advisory services" are probably linked to certain firms and consulting them costs money.

If you need to get in touch with the Universal Credit agency, try

www.gov.uk/universal-credit

or phone 0800 328 5644

DON'T try a payday loan to "Tide you over," as their interest charges may leave you more in debt than you were to start with. Most areas now have **local credit unions.** These are non- profit making co-operative groups which loan money to those in need at low rates of interest. They also work out a programme to get you back on track. If finance is not one of your problems, consider saving with them to enable them to assist others. You can read about them and find your local one through Martin Lewis' (TV money expert) website

www.moneysavingexpert.com/loans/credit-unions

or just mention it when you talk to the Citizens Advice Bureau.

WILLS

This is a specialist area and if there is a problem you may need a solicitor. They charge for an initial consultation, so again, talk to the citizens advice bureau first. Don't forget that when the dust settles, you may need to make a new will of your own. You may find more help at

www.supportline.org.uk/problems/bereavement

which offers confidential support for those in difficult circumstances.

Unfortunately, some of the legal and financial matters need dealing with fairly urgently, just when you are least able to cope. A trusted friend or family member may be able to help, or if not, I would definitely consult the local branch of your bank.

FILLING THE EMPTINESS

You may have given up your job and your interests to be your loved one's full time carer. All this has now turned to a hollow emptiness.

If your job was merely put on hold, you may be able to return to it. Give yourself a rest and a breathing space before you take up the reins again. Be aware that the place will have moved on without you. Treat it as going into a new job. New relationships and pecking orders will need to be established. Take your time, and don't panic. If systems have changed, it won't endear you to anyone to keep saying WE always used to…

What if you can't face it or you are too old to work? Sort out the finances first (as in "Practical Problems) can you **afford** to stay at home? Would a part time job be enough? Try your local job centre or this website:

www.gov.uk/find-a-job

If you are definitely not going to work then this is the time to plan, not just drift aimlessly. One of the first things to consider is **fitness.**

There are seated exercise classes and specific gym classes for older people or those with certain illnesses. Your GP should be able to put you in touch. They may even offer you free sessions to get you started. Many areas now have walking clubs. If you are already fit, try longer walks or runs for charity. These activities also carry the added benefit of meeting other people but in the open air and in a socially distanced way.

Positives.

Even in tragic circumstances there may be something useful to you. It may just be that you don't have to put up with certain TV programmes anymore. Perhaps foods you were once fond of but your partner disliked could now be back on the menu. Above all, be kind to yourself. A little treat works wonders. Don't overspend, though. Now is definitely time to rethink use of spare time and hobbies.

Kit the shed out as a man cave. Start a woodwork or DIY project. Try arts and crafts

hobbies. Beware, this can run away with cash so check finances carefully first. You may find some materials in charity shops where someone may have abandoned the hobby you want to take up.

If you aren't familiar with modern technology, why not get into a local beginner's class? They usually provide equipment to learn on whilst you are there and advise on cheap second-hand stuff for home. If you were able to use the new technology you may be better able to keep in touch with family and friends.

You may have had several years of being a carer and hardly getting out. Making new friends is quite difficult unless you are naturally brash and outgoing. Volunteering to help at local charity shops or similar, helps others and is a good way to meet people. If you offer to help in your local school or hospital you will be asked to fill in a Disclosure and Barring Service form to protect those who are vulnerable.

Or, try the U3A (University of the Third Age…Not as high powered as it sounds). It offers a huge range of activities and operates in most areas. Contact **webmaster@eastmidlandsu3as.org.uk** or ask at your local library to be put in touch with them. They would also know about local book clubs if your tastes run that way.

Local churches, too, often run friendship or luncheon clubs. Most of these things will have been on hold during the Covid 19 lockdown but watch out for them starting again. All these give ideal opportunities to make new friends and forge a new way of life. If you feel too shy to cope remember the person next to you is shyer and is longing for you to speak first!

CLEAN SWEEP OR SHRINE?

There is a museum in Worksop called "Mr. Straw's House." He was a business- man in the town, living with his mother and brother. After their mother died, they changed nothing in the house until they in turn were gone. From the gravy salt and other tins in the kitchen, to the layers of scented soap and newspaper preserving her bedding, all remained as it was. For lovers of history it is a treasure trove, but would I fancy living like that for thirty years? No. It is an extreme example, but it is what some people try to do when someone very close dies.

My mother lived with us for fifteen years until she went into a care home for the final few weeks. I could not bear to see her favourite chair empty by the fireplace, so I sold it and rearranged the furniture.

Remembering those feelings, I began to reorganize the house as soon as Jim went into hospital and from there to a nursing home. The TV and CD player which I took to him were eventually left for other residents. Some clothes, paintings and other belongings went to his family or were sold. I kept just a few precious mementos, paintings and photographs.

The photos were a great help. Going through them helped me to fix an image in my mind of Jim when he was strong and healthy, not the gaunt and twisted semi-skeleton the illness made him.

The grave or where the ashes are scattered can be a focal point for grief. There may be a compulsion to tend it every day and take flowers regularly. If this is your experience and others worry about you, especially if it is difficult to reach the memorial, consider lengthening the time between visits. I needed help to get to my family graves and Jim's grave so I have found a solution which has worked especially well for me in when I cannot visit them.

I bought a little resin block containing a flower vase and with some nice words on it. (Less than £20) It sits on a raised bed in my back garden and I can put flowers in it easily when I wish.

A shelf or corner of a desk indoors would do just as well for a little personal memorial. Find a way that works for you. Try to find your own balance between remembering the past while planning for the future and living the best way you can in the present.

None of this is easy, but perhaps you may be able to claw your way back to some kind of life.

Printed in Great Britain
by Amazon